A Brief Description of Heretics
by Ephraim Pagitt

Also added to this book is a sermon,
The Nature and Danger of Heresies,
by Obadiah Sedgwick

A Brief Description of Heretics
By Ephraim Pagitt

Edited and updated by C. Matthew McMahon and Therese B. McMahon
Transcribed by Leanne Carter

Published by Puritan Publications
A Ministry of A Puritan's Mind
4101 Coral Tree Circle #214
Coconut Creek, FL 33073
www.puritanshop.com
www.apuritansmind.com
www.puritanpublications.com

This Print Edition, 2013
Electronic Edition, 2013
Manufactured in the United States of America

ISBN: 978-1-62663-021-5
eISBN: 978-1-62663-020-8

The front cover is a depiction of the Synod of Dordt condemning the heresy of Arminianism.

TABLE OF CONTENTS

MEET EPHRAIM PAGITT

Ephraim Pagitt[1] (1575-1647) was born in Northamptonshire, in the year 1575, and educated in Christ's college, Oxford. He was the son of Mr. Eusebius Pagitt, a celebrated puritan divine, and a great sufferer for nonconformity. He was so great a proficient in the knowledge of the languages,[2] that upon his admittance into the university, the Greek professor sought his acquaintance, and derived much assistance from him. At the age of twenty-six years, he understood and wrote fifteen or sixteen languages (*cf.* Paget's *Heresiography*, Preface, 1662). Having completed his studies at the university, he became minister at St. Edmund's church, Lombard street, London, where he continued many years. While in this situation, he entered into the conjugal state, and married Lady Bord, widow of Sir Stephen Bord, of a worthy family in Sussex. Upon the commencement of the civil wars, he was a great sufferer; and he was so much troubled and molested, Mr. Wood says, that, merely for the sake of

---

[1] Taken from Benjamin Brook's *Lives of the Puritans*, Volume 3, 1813 Edition, (pages 62-63).
[2] Foulis' *Hist. of Plots*, p. 183, 181. Clarendon's *Hist.* vol. i. p. 184.

quietness, he left his benefice in his old age, being then commonly called old father Ephraim.[3] He retired to Deptford in Kent, where he spent the remainder of his days in retirement and devotion. He entered into the joy of his Lord in the month of April, 1647, aged seventy-two years. His remains, according to his last will and testament, were laid in Deptford churchyard.

Though his name is enrolled among the sufferers in the royal cause, he is with justice classed among the puritans. Many excellent divines, who were dissatisfied with the ecclesiastical discipline and ceremonies, and even with episcopacy itself, were nevertheless, during the national confusions, great sufferers on account of their loyal attachment to his majesty and the civil constitution. Their zeal for the king and his cause exposed them to the severity of the opposite party. This appears to have been the case with Mr. Pagitt. He was decided in his attachment to his majesty's interest and the civil constitution, for which he was a sufferer in those evil times; yet he was opposed to the ecclesiastical establishment, as well as the cruel oppressions of the prelates. Therefore, in the year 1645, being only two years before his death, he united with

---

[3] Wood's *Athene Dion.* Vol. ii. p. 51.

his brethren, the London ministers, in presenting a petition to the lords and commons in parliament, for the establishment of the Presbyterian discipline. Being a Presbyterian, he wrote with great bitterness against the independents, baptists, and other sectaries, by which he exposed himself to the resentment of his enemies. "Error and heresy," it is said, "began to take deep root, and to spread far and wide over the face of the earth; he, therefore, set himself to discover them, and root them up, when he published his "Heresiography." Hence sprung his trouble."[4] It is also added, "the enemies of goodness making that the ground of their malice, which he wrote to undeceive and bring them into the way of truth. Upon this he was persecuted, reviled, slandered, and, through false suggestions, suffered even imprisonment itself. He bore up manfully, and suffered patiently whatever their malice could inflict, till at last the Lord in mercy put an end to his misery, and received him to himself." He was an excellent preacher, and his sermons were as pleasant as they were profitable, drawing the hearts of his auditors, as by a bait of pleasure, to that which is good.[5]

---

[4] Grey's *Examination*, vol. ii. Appen. p. 87-89.
[5] Pagitt's *Heresiography*, Pref. Edit. 1662.

His works are, aside from various sermons:

1. *Christianographie: or, a Description of the multitudes and sundry sorts of Christians in the world not subject to the Pope,* 1635.

2. *A Treatise of the Ancient Christians in Kritany,* 1640.

3. *Heresiographie: or, a Description of the Heresies of later Times,* 1645.

4. *The Mystical Wolf,* a Sermon on Matt. 7:15, 1645.

INTRODUCTION

This is a brief collection out of Master Pagitt's book called Heresiography, or, a description of the heretics and sects of these latter times. The larger work is extensive, but this work covers the essential doctrines and teachings of the following heretics and sectaries:

1. Jesuits

2. Socinians

3. Arminians

4. Arians

5. Adamites

6. Libertines

7. AntiScripturians

8. Soulsleepers

9. Anabaptists

10. Familists

11. Expectants and Seekers

12. Divorcers

13. Pelagians

14. Millenaries (or Millenialists)

15. AntiSabatarians

16. AntiTrinitarians

17. Sabatarians

18. Separatists

19. Apostolics or Charismatics

20. Antinomians

If the reader desires to read more of these sects, he should take up the larger work by Mr. Pagitt's book which covers, in depth, every title in this short work.

This brief compendium is a relation of heresies, describing the original ring leaders of the same, and the time when they first began to spread, with a discovery of those described in our times.

His original work was printed in London, and sold by William Lee in Fleetstreet, published in the year 1646.

JESUITS

The original of these was named Loyola, a Spanish soldier. They bear the name of Jesus, but came from the Devil, the Father of Lies.

This order was confirmed by Paul, the third Bishop of Rome, in the year 1540.

Their errors are many, but the chief are these, *namely:*

1.   They presumptuously arrogate to themselves the name of Jesus, a name above all names, and their chief general equal with Christ.

2.   These chiefly maintain the Pope's temporal power, as well as his spiritual, by which he may depose kings.

3.   They deny the oath of allegiance.

4.   They teach that it is not only lawful to murder Christian kings, but that this is deserving of merit also.

5.   The Jesuits teach and maintain that the Pope only is *Jure Divino*, a Bishop, and that all others hold from him.

SOCINIANS

Socianismo was so named from Lelius Socinus in Master Calvin's time, his opinions are revealed through letters and correspondence.

First concerning God.

1.   That there is no natural knowledge of God by which to instant men to acknowledge or believe the Deity.

2.   That the incarnation of Christ is repugnant to reason, and can no way sufficiently be proved out of Scripture.

3.   That Christ is not truly God, and that the belief of his divine nature is not agreeable to Scripture.

4.   That Christ did not by his death satisfy for our sins.

5.   That the Holy Ghost is not God.

6.   That it is not repugnant to the word of God to believe three persons and one God.

7.   That man in the state of innocence was not created in original righteousness.

8.   That the Old Testament is not necessary for a Christian man, though it may be profitable to read.

ARMINIANS

So called from James Arminius of Leydon in the low countries in the year 1605.

The errors concerning Predestination:

1.   That in complete and not preemptory election of singular persons is made by reason of foreseen faith, repentance, sanctity and godliness, that this is the gracious and evangelical worthiness, by which he that is chosen becomes more worthy than he that is not chosen. And therefore that faith, the obedience of faith, sanctity, godliness and perseverance, are not the fruits, or effects, of the unchangeable election to glory, but conditions and causes, without which a thing is not brought to pass before required and foreseen, as already performed by those who are completely to be chosen.

2.   That all election to salvation is not unchangeable, but that some are elected, withstanding God's decree, may perish, and forever do.

3.   That in this life there is no fruit, nor sense or certainty of immutable election to glory, but on condition, contingent and mutable.

4.   That it is absurd to make an uncertain certainty that God, out of his mere just will, has not decreed to leave any man in the fall of Adam and common state of sin and damnation, or to pass over any in the communication of grace necessary to faith and conversion.

5.   That the reason God sends the Gospel to one nation rather than another is not the mere and only good pleasure of God, but because such a nation is better and more worthy of the Gospel.

Further concerning the death of Christ and his redemption.

1.   That God ordained first his Son to death on the cross without any certainty or determinate counsel to save any particular man expressly, *etc.*

2.   That the will of God was not to establish a new covenant of grace by the blood of Christ, but to procure the making again with men any covenant, either of grace or works.

3.   That Christ by his death did not certainly merit for any man's salvation itself, and faith by which this satisfaction of Christ may be fully applied to salvation, *etc.*

4.   That the covenant of grace, which the Father, by the mediation of the death of Christ, made with men, does not consist of their being justified before God, and saved by faith in apprehending the merit of Christ, but in this, the exaction of perfect legal obedience being abrogated, reputes faith in itself, and the imperfect obedience of faith for the perfect obedience of the law.

5.   That all men are received into the state of reconciliation and grace of the covenant, and none condemned for original sin.

6.   That Christ neither did nor ought to die for those whom God dearly loved, and chose to eternal life, seeing such stood in no need of Christ's death.

There are many other errors and heresies that the Arminians hold, concerning man's corruptions, conversions, and the perseverance of the saints.

ARIANS

These are so called from Arius, deacon of the Church of Alexandria, who infected the world with this heresy, and was condemned by 318 bishops at the Council of Nicea under the Emperor Constantine the Great, and was banished.

1.   They deny the Trinity of persons in the Godhead.

2.   They deny the Son to be God.

3.   They deny the eternal generation of the Son, which is, they say, against reason and truth.

4.   They deny Christ to be called God in respect to his essence, but by reason of his dominion.

5.   They deny the Holy Spirit to be God.

These heretics have been burned among us before now, as on March 18, 1611. One Bartholomew Legate, and the April following, one Edward Whightman, burned at Litchfield for the same.

ADAMITES

Of this heresy Saint Augustine makes mention.

1.   They call the place of their meeting Paradise.
2.   They pray, hear, and celebrate the communion naked according to the similitude of Adam before his fall.

But more lately practiced by a Piccard in Bohemia that came out of the Low Countries, and professed himself to be the Son of God, he taught this sect to go naked, and to call him Adam, terming him and his sect freemen, and all the rest slaves that wear clothes.

LIBERTINES

Libertines are those that would abolish the Law. The author of these by Pontanus is described to be one John Agricola who spread this opinion in the year 1585. The particulars of this are as *follows:*

1.   That the Law was not given to Christian men.

2.   The Law pertains to the wicked, not to the godly.

3.   The Ten Commandments do not need to be taught in the church because they that are regenerate do not need the Law, because they do that duty willingly, being led by the Spirit.

4.   That there is no need of the Law in conjunction with any part of our conversion.

5.   It is sufficient for a wicked man to believe and not doubt of his salvation.

6.   Faith and the Gospel were unknown to Moses.

7.   That good works cannot avail for salvation, neither evil works hinder.

8.   That a Christian man cannot be known by his works.

9.   That the rule of the Law is not a rule of life.

ANTISCRIPTURIANS

Antiscripturians of old, mentioned by a judicious Divine.

The heretics that lived in former times raised up from the pit of hell by Satan himself to disturb and destroy the faith of many, have called various books of these holy Scriptures into question, and rejected them altogether as bastards and counterfeits.

1.   Faustus in the Manichee, as Saint Augustine witnessed, was not ashamed to open his blasphemous mouth and affirm that many things in the New Testament were false.

2.   The Ebionites would receive only the Gospel according to Matthew; the other three they despised and refuted.

3.   The Marchionites, another detestable and damned sect, used only Luke's Gospel, and that also they miserably mangled, according to their own devilish fancy.

4.   The Tacians and other heretics, called Serveriani, as Eusebius makes mention of in his history,

saw no importance in the Acts of the Apostles and Paul's Epistles.

5.   Marcion and Basilides, refused both the Epistles to Timothy, as well as to Titus and the Hebrews, for whatsoever they saw to cross or contradict their heresies, they razed out of the Canon, and would not receive it as authentic, so that some have renounced the Epistle to the Hebrews, some the latter Epistle of Peter, some the Epistle of James, some the Epistle to Timothy and Titus, and others the two latter familiar Epistles of John as not agreeing with their heresies.

ANTISCRIPTARIANS OF OUR TIMES

1.   That the Scriptures cannot be said to be the word of God, because there is no word but Christ, *etc.*

2.   That the Scriptures are insufficient and uncertain, and they are not an infallible rule of faith, *etc.*

3.   That the penmen of Scripture, every one, wrote as they themselves conceived. They were the actions of their own spirits which moved them to write and speak.

4.   That the Scriptures of the Old Testament do not concern nor bind Christians under the New.

5.   That right reason is the rule of faith, and we are to believe all the Scriptures so far as they are agreeable to reason.

SOUL SLEEPERS

1.   That the soul dies with the body, and all things shall have an end except God.

2.   That the soul dies with the body, and was held in the time of Origen in Arabia, much extinguished by his dispute presently after the birth: this opinion is now raised again among us, and endeavored to be maintained in a treatise lately published, entitled Man's Mortality. One argument is out of Gen. 3:19, where it is said Adam shall return to dust again. I shall here end with particulars, because historians mention few others, and descend to our times.

(Some of our historians mention a few others before we come to the present time.)

ANABAPTISTS

The chief author of the errors held by these Anabaptists about the year 1524 was according to Melanchthon, one Nicholas Storke, after much pains of preaching by Doctor Luther in Saxony, and by a scholar of Storke's much dispersed, if the story is true, the practice of these opinions included monstrous cruelty.

The ancient errors of these Anabaptists recorded by Bullinger and others in the church, are these:

1.   That Christ did not assume his flesh and blood from the Virgin Mary.

2.   That Christ is not truly God, but only endued with more gifts than other men.

3.   Our righteousness does not depend upon faith in Christ, but upon the works of Charity and Affliction.

4.   They deny the doctrine of original sin and those that depend upon the same.

5.   They deny baptism to infants, because they are not capable of faith and repentance.

6.   They rebaptize those that were baptized in their infancy.

7.   They hold that before the day of judgment, the wicked should be destroyed and only the godly should reign alone.

8.   They teach free will in spiritual things.

9.   They separate from all other men as impure.

10.   That laymen may preach and administer sacraments.

Errors in the Commonwealth.

1.   That it is unlawful for a Christian man to be a magistrate.

2.   That it is unlawful to punish any offender with death.

3.   That a Christian man cannot with a safe conscience take an oath.

4.   That it is unlawful to take up arms for laws and civil liberties.

Errors in Families.

1.   That a Christian may not possess anything proper to himself, but what he has ought to be common.

2.   That a wife of a contrary religion may be put away.

FAMILISTS

The author of this sect is more lately described to appear since 1600, which was one David George of Delph; after him one Henry Nicholas, born in Amsterdam.

1.   Concerning God, that there is no other deity belonging to God, but that which men are partakers of in this life.

2.   Concerning Christ, (a) that Christ is not God, (b) that Christ is not one man, but a state and condition in men.

3.   Of Adam, that Adam was all that God was, and God all that Adam was.

4.   Of baptism, that none should be baptized until he was thirty years of age.

5.   Concerning the word, that there was never truth preached since the apostles' time until Henry Nicholas.

6.   Concerning the resurrection, (a) the resurrection of the body is a rising from sin and wickedness, (b) that the dead shall rise and live in

Henry Nicholas and the illuminated elders everlastingly, and reign upon the earth.

7.   Concerning the day of judgment, (a) that the day of judgment is in this life, (b) that the joys of heaven are upon the earth.

8.   Concerning marriage, that the marriages of those who are not enlightened with true faith are filthy and polluted.

9.   Concerning Henry Nicholas, (a) that he is raised from the dead, (b) he can no more err than Moses or Christ, (c) he is the true prophet of God sent to blow the last trumpet of doctrine which shall be published upon the earth, (d) that he only knows the true sense of Scripture, (e) that his books are of equal authority with Scripture, (f) that the Scriptures are fulfilled in Henry Nicholas and his family, (g) Henry Nicholas knows the secrets of our hearts, (h) that all men must submit to him.

10.   Concerning the illuminated elders and family, (a) all illuminated elders are *godded* with God (or deified); and God in them are hominified (or become man), (b) the disciples are Adams, and the illuminated elders are Christ, (c) the eldest father of the family is Christ himself, (d) that the estate of all who are not of

this sect are false beings, the antichrist, the wicked spirit, the kingdom of hell, the devil himself, (d) the family of love is perfect in this life, and therefore ought not to pray for forgiveness of sin, (e) that their illuminated elders do not sin, (f) that they may join with any congregation and live in any state under any magistrate in obedience though never so ungodly, (g) whatsoever is taught by any other than their illuminated elders is false.

11.   Concerning their congregation, (a) he that is one of them is perfect as Christ, (b) that it is lawful to do whatsoever the higher power commands, (c) it is ridiculous to say "God the Father, God the Son and God the Holy Ghost," for in saying so, they affirm three Gods, (d) that every man must first be in an error before he can come to the knowledge of the truth, (e) that heaven and hell are present in this world, and that there is none other, (f) that they are bound to give alms to none but of their sect, (g) that they ought not to bury their dead, because it is said, "Let the dead bury their dead," (h) that none ought to receive the sacrament before he receives the whole ordinances, to be admitted with a kiss, then his feet must be kissed, *etc.*, (i) they should not to say David's Psalms as prayers

without sin, (j) that there ought to be no Sabbath day, but all days alike, (k) that the Law of God is possible to be kept, (l) that it is expedient to manifest their whole hearts with all their counselors, minds and will together, with their thoughts and doings, and exercises, bare and naked, and not to cover or hide anything before the children of love.

1.   That there is but one spirit or life in all creatures both in heaven, earth and hell, and that life, which is one, and the fame in all creatures, is absolutely and essentially God.

2.   That all things whatsoever are the act of God; that all creatures, angels and men are at all times, in all works, acted and ruled by the Spirit of God.

3.   That nothing shall remain to eternity, but shall perish and come to nothing, except for the deity that is now the life of all creatures.

4.   That the Bible is a mere shadow, a false history, confused, being an allegory, being of no more authority than any other book or the Apocrypha.

5.   They hold that all ordinances are but meat for babes, and that we should live above them and without the use of them.

6.   That perfection in the highest degree both of grace and glory is to be enjoyed in this life.

Expectants and Seekers.

1.   That there is no church or ordinances, nor ministry in the world.

2.   That it is the will of God that miracles should attend the ministry, as in the primitive times.

DIVORCERS

These are those that will put away their wives for small offenses, not regarding the word of our Savior in Matthew 19:9, that whosoever shall put away his wife, except it be for whoredom, commits adultery, and whosoever marries her that is divorced commits adultery.

PELAGIANS

This heresy comes from Pelagius, a Welsh man. In Welsh his name was Morgan, which signifies the sea; he lived in the year 416, in the time of the Emperor Theodosius the younger. He was condemned in the Synod of Carthage in the year 423, in which were assembled 217 bishops, Saint Augustine among them. His errors are reported to be these:

1.   That Adam had died although he had not sinned by the law of nature, and so sin was not the cause of death.

2.   Adam's sin was only noxious to himself, and not to his posterity, and that there was no original sin.

3.   Lust and concupiscence were natural, not evil, but rather good, and that sin was not propagated by generation.

4.   Children have no original sin from their parents.

5.   Children of the faithful, though not baptized, are saved, and enjoy everlasting life, but not in heaven.

6.   Men have free will; even after sin, they sufficiently do well without God's grace.

7.   Grace is obtained by the merit of our works.

8.   Grace in Scripture is not meant as pardon of sin, and giving of the Holy Ghost, but the promulgation of doctrine.

9.   Faith is only the knowledge of the Law and history, not a special work of perseverance.

10.   The Law of God is satisfied by eternal obedience and is not impossible for a man to keep.

MILLENIALISTS

1.   That hold to Christ's personal reign.

2.   That Christ shall come personally from heaven and reign with his saints upon the earth a thousand years before the day of judgment.

ANTRITRINITARIANS

1.   That in the unity of the Godhead, there is not a Trinity of persons, *etc.*

2.   That there are not three distinct persons in the Divine Essence, but only three distinct offices, *etc.*

3.   That Christ's human nature is defiled with original sin, as well as ours, *etc.*

ANTISABBATARIANS

That all days are alike to Christians under the New Testament, and they are bound no more to obey the first day of the week than any other.

SABBATARIANS

That the Jewish Saturday Sabbath is still to be kept by Christians.

SEPARATISTS

1.   That it is necessary to be joined in church fellowship as well as with Christ the head, and it is so necessary that there is no expectation of salvation without it.

2.   That the Church of England and the ministry thereof is anti-Christian and of the devil, and that it is absolutely sinful and unlawful to hear any of them.

APOSTOLICS OR CHARISMATICS

1.   That many Christians in these days have more knowledge than the apostles, *etc.*

2.   That there is salvation to be revealed which was unknown to the apostles themselves.

3.   That in a small time, God will raise up apostles, men extraordinarily endued with visible, infallible gifts, to preach the Gospel, *etc.*

4.   That the gift of miracles is not ceased in these times.

5.   That miracles are essential to the administration held forth in the commission of baptism.

Errors regarding free will.

1.   There is no free will in man, either for good or evil, either in his natural or glorified state.

2.   That there is a power in man to resist grace, and that the grace which would convert one man would not convert another.

3.   That regenerate men who have true grace may fall totally and finally away.

Errors regarding free grace held by Antinomians.

1.   That the moral law is of no use to believers, *etc.*

2.   That the doctrine of repentance is a soul-destroying doctrine.

3.   That there ought to be no fasting days under the Gospel.

4.   That believers do not need to take care or to look to themselves, to keep from sin, *etc.*

5.   That God loves his children the same whether sinning or praying.

Errors regarding the Resurrection.

1.   Infants do not rise again because they are not capable of knowing God and so not capable of enjoying him.

2.   That there is no resurrection at all of the bodies of men after this life, nor heaven, nor hell, or devils.

Errors regarding Christ's dying for all.

1.   That Christ died for all men alike, for the reprobate as well as the elect, not only sufficiently but effectually, *etc.*

2.   That Christ did only satisfy for the sins against the first covenant, not for the sins against the second, *etc.*

3.   Every man satisfies for himself for the sins against the second covenant, namely unbelief, *etc.*

4.   That men may be saved without Christ, and the very heathens are saved if they serve God according to that knowledge God has given them, though they never heard of Christ.

5.   That there is no original sin in us, only Adam's first sin was original.

6.   That the guilt of Adam's sin is imputed to no man.

NEW ERRORS TENDING TO LIBERTINISM

1.   That God has a hand in, and is the author of, the sinfulness of his people.

2.   That it is the will and command of God, that since the coming of his Son, a permission to worship to the most pagan, Jewish, Turkish or anti-Christian consciences and worship, be granted to all men in all nations and countries.

3.   That no man was cast into hell for any sin, but only if God would have it so.

4.   That man had life before God breathed into him, and that which God breathed into him was part of the Divine Essence, and shall return to God again.

5.   That the Prince of the Air that rules the children of disobedience is God, and that there is no other spirit but one, and that Spirit is God.

6.   That God has not decreed all the actions of men, because men doing what God decreed do not sin.

7.   That God was never displeased with men, for if he were, and then were pleased again, there is a changeableness in God.

8.   That God does not love one man more than another before the world, neither is there any particular election, but only general and conditional, the Scriptures nowhere speaking of reprobates or reprobation.

There are many more recited by Master Edwards and Master Pagitt and others. But this is not the only way to decrease errors, by a violent, furious repetition of them. A discovery of fewer errors solidly refuted, will, if done in the spirit of love, prove a better employment than to discover hundreds and spend nothing but wrath and fleshly, carnal censures on them. Certainly it would be far more acceptable to God and Jesus Christ to turn someone that is going on in an error, than to discover one hundred for him to fall into. It is a great sin in many to pry into God's secrets; and it is as great a sin also in many to set too high a price on ignorance. I shall end with these Scripture admonitions, desiring that they may be more seriously thought on than they are yet by both parties.

"But if ye have bitter envying and strife in your hearts, glory not, and lie not against the truth," (James 3:14).

"This wisdom descendeth not from above, but is earthly, sensual, devilish. For where envying and strife is, there is confusion and every evil work. But the wisdom that is from above is first pure, then peaceable, gentle, and easy to be intreated, full of mercy and good fruits, without partiality, and without hypocrisy. And the fruit of righteousness is sown in peace of them that make peace, (James 3:15-18).

ORDINANCE

The heads of an ordinance, presented to the Honorable House of Commons, by Mr. Bacon, a lawyer in Suffolk, and Master Tate, both of them members of the same House, and by their means was read twice and referred to a committee. This is for the preventing and of the growing and spreading of heresies.

Let it be ordained, that all who shall from this day and after willingly preach, teach, print or write, publish and maintain any such opinion contrary to the doctrines following:

These are, that God is present in all places, that God is, or that he is one in three Persons, or knows or foreknows all things, or that he is Almighty, or that he is perfectly holy, or that he is eternal; Or that shall in like manner publish that Christ is not God, equal with the Father, or shall deny the manhood of Christ, or that the Godhead and manhood of Christ are several natures, or that the manhood of Christ is pure, unspotted by sin; Or that shall publish that Christ did not die, or rise from the dead nor is ascended into Heaven bodily; Or that his death is meritorious in behalf of believers; Or that shall publish or maintain, as said before, that Christ is not the Son of God, or that the Holy Ghost is not God, or that the scriptures are not the Word of God, or that the bodies of men shall not rise after they are dead, or that there is no day of judgment after death.

Such publishing with obstinacy shall be judged felony. Such persons shall by two witnesses be bound over by two justices to the jail delivery, and the delinquent shall be indicted for felony. And on finding the same indictment, and that party be found guilty, and shall not abjure his said error, he shall suffer the pains of death without benefit of clergy. But on abjuring of the said error, he shall upon two sufficient sureties be bailed.

And let it be further ordained, that if after abjuring the said errors, he shall publish it again, he shall be indicted and put to death.

And let it be further ordered, that if any person shall wittingly and presumptuously, or contrary to admonition, blaspheme the name of God, or any of the

Holy Trinity, or shall impugn the word of God, such offenses shall be judged a felony, and the offender committed without bail. And the party being found guilty shall be branded in the left cheek with the letter B and on the same offense the second time shall suffer death.

And be it further ordained that all persons who shall publish any of the following errors:

> That all men shall be saved; that a man by nature has free will to turn to God; that God may be worshipped by pictures or images; or that the soul of any man after death goes neither to heaven nor hell, but to Purgatory; or that the soul of man dies or sleeps when the body is dead; or that the revelations or workings of the Spirit are a rule for a Christian's life, though varying from or contrary to the written Word of God; or that a man is bound to believe no more than by his reason he can comprehend; or that the moral law contained in the Ten Commandments is no rule of a Christian's life; or that God sees no sin in the justified; or that a believer need not repent nor pray for the pardon

of sin; or that the two sacraments of baptism and the Lord's Supper are not ordinances commanded by the Word of God; or that the baptizing of infants is unlawful, or that such baptizing is void and of none effect, or that such persons are to be baptized again, and in pursuance thereof, shall baptize any person formerly baptized; or that the observation of the Lord's Day, as it is enjoined by the ordinances and laws of this realm, is not according or contrary to the Word of God; or that it is not lawful to join in public, or family, prayer, or to teach children to pray; or that the Churches of England are not true churches, or that the ministers or ordinances are not true ministers or ordinances, or that the church government by presbytery is anti-Christian or unlawful; or that the magistracy or power of the civil magistrate by law established in England is unlawful; or that all the use of arms for public defense (be the cause ever so just) is unlawful.

And in case the party accused of any of the said errors is committed before two justices, that party shall be ordered to renounce his error in the public congregation of the Parish Church from where the complaint comes; and in case he refuses or neglects the same at or upon the day, time and place appointed by the justices, he shall be committed to prison by the justices, until he shall find two sureties, of subsidy men that he shall not publish or maintain the said error or errors any more. Amen.

MEET OBADIAH SEDGWICK

Obadiah Sedgwick (1600-1658) was a Presbyterian, Reformed puritan divine. He was the son of Joseph Sedgwick, vicar of St. Peter's, Marlborough, Wiltshire, afterwards of Ogbourne St. Andrew, Wiltshire, and born at Marlborough about 1600. He attended Queen's College, Oxford, on June 18, 1619, aged 19, removed thence to Magdalen Hall, and graduated with a B.A. on May 5, 1620, and with an M.A. on Jan. 23, 1623. He was tutor (1626) to Sir Matthew Hale. Having taken orders, he became chaplain to Horatio, baron Vere of Tilbury, whom he accompanied to the Low Countries. Returning to Oxford, he commenced to gain a B.D. on Jan. 16, 1630. His first preferment (1630) in the church was as lecturer at St. Mildred's, Bread Street, London, where his puritanism got him into trouble. On July 6, 1639 he was presented by Robert Rich, second earl of Warwick, to the vicarage of Coggeshall, Essex, in succession to John Dod. On the opening of the Long parliament he regained his lectureship at St. Mildred's, and became a preacher against episcopacy. Mr. Wood says that he used to "in hot weather to unbutton his doublet in the pulpit, that his breath might be the longer." In the autumn of 1642 he was chaplain to the regiment of foot raised by Denzil Holles.

Sedgwick was a member of the Westminster Assembly (1643), and in the same year was appointed a licenser of the press. On Oct. 6, 1643 he spoke at the Guildhall in favour of the league with Scotland for the prosecution of the war, and his speech was published in "Foure Speeches," 1646, 4to. In a sermon of September 1644 he preached for "cutting off delinquents." He held for a short time the rectory of St Andrew's, Holborn, on the sequestration (Dec. 13, 1645) of John Hacket; but next year (before May, 1646) he was appointed to the rectory of St. Paul's, Covent

Garden, and resigned Coggeshall where John Owen (1616-1683) succeeded him (August 18). He was a member of the eleventh London classis in the parliamentary Presbyterianism; but his ecclesiastical views were not rigid, for on March 20, 1654 he was appointed one of Cromwell's "triers," and in August of the same year was a clerical assistant to the "expurgators." His health failing, he resigned St Paul's in 1656, and was succeeded by his son-in-law, Thomas Manton. He was a man of property, being lord of the manor of Ashmansworth, Hampshire. Retiring to Marlborough, he died there at the beginning of January 1658, and was buried near his father, in the chancel of Ogbourne St. Andrew, A portrait of Sedgwick, engraved by W. Richardson, is mentioned by Bromley. By his wife Priscilla he had a son Robert, baptized at Coggeshall on Oct. 19, 1641, who was a frequent preacher before parliament, and published many sermons between 1639 and 1657.

Besides these and a catechism, he published: 1. "Christ's Counsell to...Sardis," 1640, 8vo. 2. "The Doubting Believer," 1641, 12mo; 1653, 12mo. 3. "The Humbled Sinner," 1656, 4to; 1660, 4to. 4. "The Fountain

Opened," 1657, 4to. 5. "The Riches of Grace," 1657, 12mo; 1658, 12mo.

Posthumous (after his death) were: 6. "The Shepherd of Israel," 1658, 4to. 7. "The Parable of the Prodigal," 1660, 4to. 8. "The Anatomy of Secret Sins," 1660, 4to. 9. "The Bowels of Tender Mercy," 1661, fol.

For Further study:

Mr. Wood's Athenæ Oxon. (Bliss), in, 65, 442, 1090, iv. 751; Mr. Wood's Fasti (Bliss), i. 392, *etc.*; Foster's Alumni Oxon, 1892, iv. 1331; Baxter's Reliquiae, 1696, i. 42; Walker's Sufferings of the Clergy, 1714, ii. 171; Brook's Lives of the Puritans, 1813, ii. 485 sq., iii. 295 sq.; Neal's Hist. of the Puritans (Toulmin), 1822, vol. iii.; Dale's Annals of Coggeshall, 1863, pp. 155 sq.; Mitchell and Struthers's Minutes of Westminster Assembly, 1874, p. 219 sq.

THE NATURE AND DANGER

OF HERESIES

Opened in a Sermon before the Honorable House of Commons, January 27, 1646 at Margaret's, Westminster, being the day of their Solemn Monthly Fast.

by Obadiah Sedgwick, B.D.
Minister of God's Word at Covent-Garden

"But there were false prophets also among the people, even as there shall be false teachers among you, who privily shall bring in damnable heresies, even denying the Lord that bought them, and bring upon themselves swift destruction," (2 Peter 2:1).

"Ye therefore, beloved, seeing ye know these things before, beware lest ye also, being led away with the error of the wicked, fall from your own steadfastness. But grow in grace, and in the knowledge of our Lord and Saviour Jesus Christ. To him be glory both now and for ever. Amen," (2 Peter 3:17-18).

LONDON,
Printed by M.F. for Samuel Gellibrand at the
Brazen Serpent in Paul's Churchyard,
1647.

INTRODUCTION

To The Honorable House of Commons, now Assembled in Parliament:

Having received your commands to preach that which first presented itself to my thoughts was the subject of this ensuing discourse, a theme (if I understand the present posture of these times) both seasonable and necessary. There are some points of difference which are of an inferior consequence, and stand further off from the foundation, these being but *Judicia domestica*. I do not meddle with these, but there are other positions which pull hard at the very foundation, and which subvert the faith. Against these I hold it my duty as a Christian, as a minister of Christ, and as your servant, to declare it myself. And I exhort you, before whom it was more fit to open those ulcerous sores than before yourselves (Right Honorable) who, under God, are our most choice and tender physicians.

If any reader should now be so unhappy in his charity as to calumniate this discovery of heresies and blasphemies to be an arrow subtlety designed against holiness and good men, to these I would reply in the following way: 1) The surest friends to holiness have been the sharpest enemies to errors; Christ and His apostles were this way. 2) That I never yet have learned what direct advantage at any time redounded to true sanctity by a patient endurance of heresy and blasphemy. 3) Nor can I be so uncharitable as to think that any person sincerely holy, or intending the progress of holiness, dares to be a friend to such damnable and soul-destroying errors. The design which I would commend to all in this time of reformation is this: that truth and holiness (which are so naturally combined and so mutually interested), may be conscientiously promoted with equal zeal. Encourage holiness, but contend for the truth too. Maintain the truth, but countenance holiness too.

He who pretends holiness but does not regard truth, and he who pretends the truth but does not regard holiness, neither of these is a cordial friend either to truth or holiness. Right Honorable, be pleased to go on (as you have begun) in the strenuous support of them both. Both of them have a necessary respect to God's glory. Both of them have a necessary respect to man's salvation. Both of them have a necessary respect to our present reformation. Both of them will prove the kingdom's safety, your conscience's comfort, and the crown of all your long and great labors. For both of these, you have the prayers of,

Your most unworthy, yet most faithful servant,
OBADIAH SEDGWICK

THE SERMON

"And the serpent cast out of his mouth water as a flood after the woman, that he might cause her to be carried away of the flood. And the earth helped the woman, and the earth opened her mouth, and swallowed up the flood which the dragon cast out of his mouth," (Revelation 12:1516).

This text is a seasonable text, seasonable to the times in which we live and seasonable to the work of this day, which should be humbling work and reforming work. The parts of the text are two: a renewed danger, verse 15, and a renewed succor, verse 16.

I. THE NEW DANGER IS SET FORTH IN FOUR PARTICULARS

1.   By its author [*and the serpent*]. There is a former danger mentioned in verses 12-13. That was managed by the wrathful dragon; and here is a new danger, which is contrived by the cunning serpent. Open cruelty is more

dreadful, but subtle policy is more pernicious. The cunning devil is a more mischievous enemy to the Church of Christ than the raging devil. Nero and Diocletian were sore enemies to the Church, but of all the Emperor Julian is reputed the worst.

2.   By its engine [*the serpent cast out of his mouth*]. It is a question among the schoolmen whether *peccata oris* (mouth sins) may not be worse than *peccata operis* (sins of work). I am sure that the danger which comes out of the mouth of the serpent far exceeds that danger which depends upon the sword of the dragon.

There is a mouth of truth, and that is God's mouth. There is a mouth of peace, and that is Christ's mouth. There is a mouth of prayer, and that is a good man's mouth. There is a mouth of cursing, and that is the wicked man's mouth. There is a mouth of mischief, and that is the serpent's mouth. When the devil wrecked Adam and Eve, he used the mouth of the serpent; and when he deceived Ahab, he became a lying spirit in the mouth of the false prophets. When he would deceive the whole world, he falls into the mouth of the beast to speak great things. And here, intending to destroy the Church, he uses the mouth of the serpent.

3.   By its matter [*and the serpent cast out of his mouth water as a flood*]. It is not said that he cast out water only (and yet even that dropping out of the mouth of a serpent has been sufficiently dangerous), but he cast out water as a flood. Floods in Scripture are the paraphrases of the most extreme dangers. When the danger is sudden, high, violent, and quick, then it is expressed by the metaphor of a flood. David speaks of floods of ungodly men in Psalm 18:4. The prophet speaks of the enemy coming in like a flood, (Isaiah 59:19).

4.   By its scope or intention [*that he might cause the woman to be carried away of the flood*]. There was a flood which bore up the ark, but here is a flood to overwhelm and drown the ark. Whichever way the devil and his angels attempt against the Church of Christ, no less than its utter ruin is still the aim and project. When the devil rages like a dragon, his intent is utterly to waste; and, when he acts as a serpent, then his design is utterly to sink the Church.

II. SO YOU SEE THE CHURCH'S NEW DANGER; BUT NOW BEHOLD THE CHURCH'S RENEWED SUCCOR.

And, indeed, it is very remarkable that this chapter is as full of succors as it is of dangers. In verse 7, you may read of the dragon and his angels appearing in the field and fighting, but then you read of Michael and his angels succoring even to victory in verses 8-9. Again, in verse 14, you find the dragon persecuting the woman which brought forth the man child, but then also you read that there was given to the woman two great wings of a great eagle, that she might fly into the wilderness, verse 14. And here you see a flood cast out to carry away the woman, but with it you read of a gracious and present succor: "And the earth helped the woman by opening her mouth, and swallowing up the flood which the dragon cast out of his mouth."

So, you have the distribution of the text. Now I proceed to the propositions which may be observed from it. The whole state and sum of this text may be resolved into these *three conclusions:*

1.   That the mischief which Satan cannot compass by open cruelty he will test against the Church of

Christ by subtle policy. When he fails as a dragon, then he will try what he can do as a serpent.

2.   That the serpent's flood is the chief and worst of the Church's dangers.

3.   That the Lord still has raised fresh succors for the Church against the fresh dangers of the Church.

Concerning the first of these, I intend to have demonstrated both the truth of it and its practice in all ages of the Church, as well as the several methods, wiles, stratagems, and designs of Satan on and against the Church of Christ, and the reasons of shifting his hand and making use of his mouth, of desisting from open cruelty and falling to his wiles of policy. And then, also, I intend to show the wonderful mischief that has redounded by it that, where his cruelty has killed thousands, his policy has slain ten thousands, where also might have been revealed: (1) The advantages of policy above cruelty; (2) The general receptivity or capacity in men to be taught by the policies of this serpent; (3) The usual inadvertencies rather under the workings of the serpent than of the devil; and (4) The specious ways of insinuating his mischief in the ways of policy.

But I was taken off from my purpose in handling this point (though, as to my own opinion, very necessary and excellent) because I should by it check myself in the handling of the second point, which I desired chiefly to discourse on this day before this Honorable Audience. And, therefore, omitting other things, I address myself to that proposition which shall be the only subject of my present pains. The proposition is this: The serpent's flood is the chief and worst of the Church's dangers, "The serpent cast out of his mouth a flood to carry away the woman."

Interpreters are carried away with several conjectures concerning this flood which is cast out to carry away the Church. There is a flood of tears and a flood of reproaches and slanders. That is a flood in which we should drown our sins; this is a flood in which men drown our names. And there is a flood of persecution, and a flood of invasion, and a flood of erroneous opinions, which, of these three latter it is, may be questioned.

Some, by this flood of waters, understand the flood of blood let out by the pagan emperors. A red sea was that cloud. They endeavored all they could to drown the Church in its own blood. But this opinion is not very probable because the former danger in the practices of the dragon did not comprehend this flood, and it seems clearly to be mentioned already in verse 11, where it is said, "They loved not their lives unto death."

Others, by this flood, understand the eruption of the Franks and Vandals, Huns and Longobards who, about the year 400, broke in on Asia and Europe like a tempest and a swelling inundation and, in a sort, overwhelmed the Christian world. This, I confess, was a flood, but whether it is that which is implied in the text, I greatly doubt because the text speaks of a flood cast out of the mouth of the serpent. But in the eruptions of those aforementioned people, there was neither the serpent nor the mouth. It was plain, public, notorious cruelty, managed by the hand, not a danger managed by secret subtlety and in the mouth.

The writer Viegas, by this flood, understands a strange kind of Antichrist, who shall send out his army into the wilderness and, by his satellites (surely he means some pursuivants or busy emissaries), should search caves and dens to find out the faithful, whom the earth (in a literal sense), should swallow up as it did Dathan and Abiram; but this idea is not worth confuting. Only let me subjoin this, that some interpreters fasten this flood on the true Antichrist of Rome, and, questionless, virtually it will reach him as to the practice; but whether it will reach the text as to its principal scope, I question.

But not to trouble you with more conjectures, their best interpreters I have met with unanimously expound this particular flood of waters to be those notorious errors, heresies, blasphemies, and schisms which Satan, by several instruments, cast out to the infection of the Church, and to the subversion of the faith immediately under the Christian emperors. When the Church of Christ obtained a little respite from the cruel sword and began to enjoy some breathing tranquility, then, all of a sudden, there broke out that flood of the Arian heresy (even in the time of Constantine the Great), in which the Deity of the Son of God was oppugned and blasphemed. And this flood rose so high and ran so swift that, in a short time, it overwhelmed the East, and after that the West, so that, in a manner, the whole world turned Arian. After that, another flood broke out: the Macedonian heresy, opposing the Deity of the Holy Spirit.

Soon after this the Pelagian heresy, against the whole gospel; and the Nestorian and Eutychian heresy, against the verity of the Person of Christ, which floods continued on the Church for nearly 300 years. And what mischief accrued to the Church of Christ by every one of them, you may abundantly read in Eusebius, Socrates, Euagrius, Sozomen, Theodoret, and others.

So that now we are come, in some good measure, to perceive what this flood cast out of the mouth of the serpent is: namely, erroneous, false, wicked, heretical doctrines, cast out of the mouths of corrupt and corrupting seducers, opposing the truth and endangering the very essence or being of the Church of Christ, concerning which, favor me with your patience while I show to you:

First, the nature of heresies and erroneous doctrines which the serpent cast out of his mouth.

Second, the danger of them to the Church of Christ, that they are perilous and hazardous. Third, the greatness of that danger. It is the chief and the worst. Fourth, some pertinent, useful applications of all this to us for our present humbling and reforming.

III. OF THE NATURE OF HERESIES

To find this out, you may be pleased to know that the word "heresy" admits of a threefold signification and use.

1.   Sometimes it is taken for any new and select opinion, contrary to the common and usually received opinions of other men; in which the word "heresy" may sometimes bear a good construction, Acts 24:14, "For after that way which the Jews called heresy, did Paul worship the God of his fathers."

2.   Sometimes it is taken for any false opinion whatsoever, in which a person recedes from any divine truth and, by it, ferments divisions, sects, and contentions.

3.   But strictly among divines, it is taken for some notorious, false, and perverse opinion, opposing and subverting the faith once delivered to the saints, as Jude says, or overthrowing the form of wholesome words, as Paul says. And it may be in this way described:

Heresy is an erroneous or false opinion, repugnant to and subverting the doctrine of faith revealed in the Word as necessary to salvation; and obstinately maintained and pertinaciously adhered to by a professed Christian.

To explain the definition consider the following *points*:

1)	Heresy is an erroneous opinion, *falsa sententia* (false sentence) or *falsum dogma* (false dogma, or false principle). There is a difference between an evil work and heresy. An evil work is one thing; heresy is another thing. In the work which a man does, there may be sin, very much sin, but properly there is not heresy. Erratum (a mistake) it may be, but it is not error unless it resides in the understanding.

The works of hypocrisy and of profaneness (like murder, injustice, adultery, theft, *etc.*) have much wickedness in them; but, unless these become the objects of opinion as well as practice, they are not heresies. Indeed if, beside the moral practice of them, anyone rises to an intellectual opinion that the practice of them is lawful and not repugnant to the Word of God, now such an opinion, erroneous opinion, of them may come to heresy.

Yes, let me add a little more. Though many practical works are acted that are repugnant to the conscience, yet the works, simply considered as works, are not to be reputed heresies. For then every sin against knowledge should be heresy. No, it is not light shining and working against an action or work which raises it to be a heresy, but it must be light in the Word shining against an opinion, which must denominate it to be heresy.

2)   Heresy is an erroneous opinion concerning matters of faith. There are questions and special questions (but different Greek words are used to describe the terms) as Gregory Nazianzen has well distinguished. Every erroneous opinion is not heresy. To make the erroneous opinion amount to heresy, two things must concur:

One, the error must be about faith. Although a man errs in his own opinion within the proportion of *objectum scibile* (a knowable object), as against the rules and principles of several sciences (Geometry, Astronomy, Natural Philosophy), yet this error is not heresy; for heresy is an erroneous opinion not about matters of human science, but about matters of divine faith. But, if the error is about the matters of faith revealed in the Word, such as Christ is not God or is not Man, here now the error will rise to heresy, for here is *dogma fidei* (doctrines of faith).

Another is that the error is against faith; against the faith as well as about the faith. If it is an opinion contrary to sound doctrine, overthrowing the foundation, this will make the error to be heresy. An opinion may be contrary not only to the Church of Rome, and many particular traditions, but also to the judgment of some godly men; yet it is not, therefore, a heresy. But then it is heresy when the opinion is contra *fidem traditam*, contrary to the faith, to the doctrine of faith in the Scriptures. Nevertheless, here we must carefully consider that an opinion may be said to be contrary to the faith in a double respect:

a)   One, when it is not concordant to every truth whatsoever which is revealed in the Scriptures. I do not dare to say that every error in this respect is heresy. There may be many mistakes, perhaps dissonant to the true chronology, to the exact and full history of some places, yet these are not necessarily heresies.

b)   The other is when it is repugnant to the truth, or any truth, which is necessary to salvation, and here, no doubt, the error against faith will prove to be heresy.

There may be diverse opinions, yet none of them are heresies. In the interpretation of the Scriptures, there is frequently a variety of opinions but, as long as the lines of a circumference meet in the center, as long as every one of them unites and harbors within the analogy of faith, there is no heresy though there is some variety. But then it is heresy when the opinion is adverse, is contrary to, is subversive of, the faith revealed as necessary to salvation, which opinion may be either:

Explicitly. When the error is manifestly fundamental, it expressly plucks up the foundation. It is not a problematical canvasing of a truth, but a plain gunpowder plot, an error which blows up a fundamental truth. It does not blow off the tiles of the house, but blows up the bottoms and supports of the house, like a person who denies the Godhead of Christ, redemption by Christ, or salvation by Christ. Or it may be:

Reductively. This is when the error overthrows that which, being denied and overthrown; the foundation on it, and by it, is by an inevitable necessity also denied and overthrown, or maintains that which, being maintained, a fundamental truth must necessarily and unavoidably be subverted. For example, if any person should maintain human satisfactions to be sufficient to merit and procure salvation; this error would necessarily subvert man's salvation founded on the merits of Jesus Christ only.

      3)   If the erroneous opinion is against any particular doctrinally necessary truth, even that particular error will amount to heresy. Indeed, number (if I may, so speak), is requisite to apostasy, but any particular necessity of a truth to our salvation (if opposed) is sufficient for heresy. The apostate turns his back from the whole truth. The heretic grapples with some truth, but denies other truth; and, therefore, though a person still retains an assent consonant to many truths, nay, to most truths, nay, to all except one necessary truth, yet, if his erroneous opinion is subversive of that one, his error will come to heresy.

      4)   To make the erroneous opinion to be heretical, it is necessary (as to the person who holds it), that he be a professed Christian. It is a question put by schoolmen and others whether infidels, pagans, and Jews who hold opinions contrary to and subversive of

the faith are to be reputed heretics. To which I answer that one may be called heretical *either:*

Materially, like when his opinion, for the matter and substance of it, is contrary to the faith and subversive of the foundation; or else,

a)   Formally, when not only the substance of the opinion is heretical and opposed to the Christian faith, but also it is maintained by one who has formerly engaged himself to the profession and maintenance of the faith.

In the former consideration, infidels and Jews may be reputed heretics, but, in this latter consideration, only he is so to be reputed who was reckoned among the number of Christians professing the faith. If the infidel and Jew deny Jesus Christ to be a Savior of sinners, though this is a great sin, yet it is not (strictly considered), a heresy because neither the one nor the other ever embraced or professed the gospel. But, if a Christian professing the gospel does this, in him it is heresy.

5)   But, lastly, to make up heresy, there must be obstinacy or pertinacity joined with that erroneous opinion which is contrary to the faith. He who is a heretic must adhere or inhere; he must

obstinately adhere or cleave to his erroneous opinion. I confess that it is a very quick case whether pertinacity is so essential to heresy that the opinion cannot at all be reputed heretical unless the professing Christian who holds it appears obstinate. Concerning which case, I will only deliver my opinion, submitting it to better judgments, that where the erroneous opinion appears, by natural reason, grossly and notoriously harmful to the raising of the foundation, it is heretical. Denying Jesus Christ to be the Son of God, or denying salvation by Him, such an opinion, in the very nature of it, is pernicious, ruinous, and damnable. Yet, in the ordinary way of discovery and process with heretics, I humbly conceive that pertinacity must be an ingredient to constitute the person to be heretically erroneous.

There is *infidelis*, one who never entertained or professed the faith, yet is obstinately and most violently carried against it. This man may be a persecutor, but he is not a heretic, notwithstanding his opinion and notwithstanding his obstinacy.

Again, there is *dubius in fide*, one who is doubtful in the faith. He is one who is wavering and reeling; his anchor does not fasten; he is not quite on nor quite off, but staggers and totters. The equal apprehensions of truth and falsehood so poise and balance the one against the other that he does not come up fully and determinately any way. Now, although some affirm that doubt is heresy, I dare not assert it. Thomas the apostle doubted; he was incredulous, but not heretical. Augustine says that one who doubts errs, for the man errs who approves falsehood for truth, or disallows truth for falsehood, or takes uncertain things for certain truths, or certain truths for uncertain conjectures. There is error here, but not heresy.

There is also *haereticocredens*. This is one who is rolled up, wriggled in, packed up into a dangerous error. He is misled, seduced, follows his leader; he holds that which is really contrary to the faith and destructive, yet not out of obstinacy of mind, but on an imagination of truth; not out of deliberation, but by stealth. He is utterly deceived by taking on trust. His erroneous opinion is not fortified with pertinacity, but only crept into him by his simplicity. And, therefore, being candidly dealt with and admonished, he does not contend, but yields and wheels about to the truth. As the bow, when the string is taken off, returns to its own posture again, so, upon admonition, the seduced person quits his error and submits to the faith.

But then there is the very heretic, and he is one who not only errs in his opinion, but also obstinately maintains that error. He not only holds that which is contrary to the faith, but he also holds the same with a pertinacious spirit.

But here, now, falls in that difficult and knotty question, namely, when a person is to be reputed obstinate or pertinacious in holding an error contrary to the faith. The apostle, I think, resolves us in this when he says, Titus 3:10, "A heretic after the first and second admonition, reject." So, then, when there is a due proposal of the truth manifestly revealed in the Scriptures, and yet the erroneous person adheres to his error out of a very depravity of mind, and will not suffer his understanding to be captivated to the truth, this person is pertinacious in holding his erroneous opinion and is manifestly a heretic.

Beloved! When an erroneous person maintains his opinion contrary to clear light so that he must necessarily deny the truth of God or revoke his error; or when he cannot maintain his wicked error, but he must necessarily overthrow some other article of faith which yet he would not do; or when the person does not care if he tramples down another truth to uphold his error against a former truth, makes one article a footstool to pull down another; or when the person steps from one error to a more gross one, and does not care what error he plunges himself into, so that he maintains his error; or when all solid reason is silenced. No, if reason and conscience might speak, they (concurring with the truth against his error), secretly condemn him and, having nothing to reply, he falls into proud scorns, bitter virulence, miserable shifts, surely such an erroneous person is obstinate and pertinacious in his corrupt opinion.

And thus, briefly, for the first question, which contains the nature of heresies. I now come to the second particular, which respects the danger of heresies.

IV. OF THE DANGER OF HERESIES

That heresies, or erroneous doctrines and opinions, are dangerous, cannot be so much as a scruple to any Christian upon the earth, unless he is turned into a heretic or into an atheist, for:

First, the Scriptures charge sin, perniciousness, and damnation on them. St. Paul reckons up heresies among those works of the flesh which shut persons out *from inheriting the kingdom of God*, Galatians 5:20-21. And St. Peter calls them *pernicious and damnable, and such as bring swift destruction*; and, speaking of the authors of them, he says that *their damnation slumbers not*, 2 Peter 2:13.

A man's opinion makes him sinful as well as his practice; and a man may be damned for a corrupt opinion as well as for a corrupt conversation. I will not put it to a dispute whether a sin against the rule of faith may not be far more sinful and damnable than the sin which is against the rule of life. But let it suffice for the present that if heresies and heterodoxies are such sins, are such locks as can shut up the gates of heaven against a soul, if they are such bars as can break up the doors of hell and bring damnation, surely that man is not himself who doubts whether they are dangerous or not.

Second, let us consider to what dangerous things heresies and corrupt doctrines are compared in Scripture, and by what dangerous creatures heretics and false teachers are expressed. By them you may judge whether heresies are dangerous or not.

1.   Heresies are compared in Scripture sometimes to a *gangrene* or *canker*, 2 Timothy 2:17, "Their word will eat as doth a canker." The canker is an invading ulcer, creeping from joint to joint, corrupting one part after another until, at length, it eats out the very heart and life. Sometimes they are compared to a *shipwreck*, 1 Timothy 1:19-20, "Hold faith and a good conscience, which some having put away concerning faith, have made shipwreck." In what a condition are the miserable passengers, when their ship is split asunder by the rock? All their goods are lost, and all their lives too. Christ calls them leaven; Paul calls them a bewitching; learned writers call them a leprosy, poison, fire, and tempest, and our text calls them a flood.

2.   As for heretics, they are expressed by creatures, very dangerous and hurtful. Sometimes they are called foxes, Song of Songs 2:15, "The foxes which spoil the grapes." Sometimes they are called dogs, rending dogs, Philippians 3:2, "Beware of dogs, beware of the concision." Sometimes they are called wolves, "grievous wolves which devour the flock," (Acts 20:29). Sometimes they are called mountebanks, cheaters, such as beguile unstable souls.

3.　　　　Third, Jesus Christ and His apostles give special charges and caveats against them, to take heed and beware of them, which they never would have done had they not been dangerous. Mark 8:15, "Beware of the leaven of the Pharisees." Matthew 7:15, "Beware of false prophets." Matthew 24:45, "Take heed that no man deceive you, for many shall come in My name saying, I am Christ, and shall deceive many." Philippians 3:2, "Beware of dogs, beware of evil workers, beware of the concision." 2 Peter 3:17, "Beware lest ye also, being led away with the error of the wicked, fall from your own steadfastness." Certainly, all these things clearly prove that there is a danger in them.

But that is not all. Danger is not all; there is yet more than mere danger in them, which will appear in the resolving of the third particular.

V. THE GREATNESS OF DANGER BY HERESIES

Heresies are the greatest and highest of dangers to the Church of Christ. You will imagine that the sword, prison, exile, dispersion, spoiling, torments, tortures, and the most cruel deaths which befell the

Church in the primitive times were extremely dangerous, and so they were; but yet not half as dangerous as the floods of heresies and corrupt opinions are. The Church ever gained by the former, grew more in purity, in unity, in prayer, in zeal and courage. But did it ever get so by heresies and erroneous doctrines? Not unless it was by accident and after much striving and medicine for recovery.

I will go no further than the text itself to set out to you the exceeding mischief and danger which comes by heresies and erroneous doctrines. They are, in the text, called a flood cast out of the mouth of the serpent. Now, seriously consider:

1.   They are a corrupting and defiling flood. Any flood is so; it presently defiles the pure waters, spoils the grounds, leaves filth and slime and mud behind it. But, surely, a flood that comes out of the mouth of a poisonous serpent is so; and there are four precious things which wicked errors or heresies poison, corrupt, and defile:

The first is the souls of men. And is there a more noble and choice thing in man, or belonging to man, than his soul? Our soul is of more value than the entire world; but heresies and wicked doctrines corrupt the soul, nay, many souls. It was the heavy indictment against Babylon that in her were found slaves and souls of men, Revelation 18:13. Heretics, in one place, are called "merchants," making "merchandise of you with feigned words," (2 Peter 2:3). In merchandising, there is something bought for a certain price. In this merchandise, the souls of people are bought for feigned words, for base metal, only for a corrupt error.

Every heretical opinion buys a soul or stabs a soul. It stabs the soul of him who maintains it, and still it trades on to murder more souls. It lifts off the soul from the foundation upon which the salvation of souls is built. What will become of a house whose foundation is removed? And what will become of a soul whose bottom for salvation is denied and rejected? Damnable heresies make us to deny the Lord that bought us, (2 Peter 2:1). O, what is this! What will follow on this, when a poor sinner comes to deny the Lord Jesus who bought him?

The second is the leading faculty of the soul. There is more danger to corrupt a captain than to corrupt many private soldiers, and most danger to corrupt a general who leads the whole army. It is capital, in some places, and at some times, to cast poison into the spring. This will poison all the streams. Heresies corrupt the great leader of the whole soul. The judgment of man is the general, the admiral, the shepherd, the overseer, the guide, the eye, the primary mover for the rest of the spheres in man. If the light in man is darkness, how great is that darkness? If the judgment is infected, how dangerous is that infection?

Beloved! If there is the darkness of ignorance from inapprehension in the mind, the soul, hereby, is in an ill case. If there is the darkness of misapprehension by error, it is in a worse case. But when that misguiding error befalls the leading faculty of all the soul, and this error falls pointblank against a truth necessary to the man's salvation, and, moreover, this error is stiffly adhered to by that leading judgment, it misleads and will mislead. O! now, in what a desperate condition is the whole soul by it! If it does not recover from this error, it dies because of it, and it can never be recovered until the judgment is altered. And when will that judgment be altered, which perversely affronts and rejects the light of truth, which alone can carry it off? The third is the most active faculty of the soul. They defile and corrupt the conscience. Now, this is amazingly dangerous. A wicked error is blinding while in the judgment only, but it is binding when it slips into the conscience also. It is a wrangling Sophister in that, but it is a working Jesuit in this. Diseases falling among the vital spirits are most quick and most dangerous. Errors are never more pernicious than when they drop into the conscience, for whatever engages conscience engages all, and the utmost of our all. If the conscience of man is made a party against the truth, now all that a man has and all that a man can do will be made out against the truth too. Now, the person will, with Paul, grow mad and desperate against Christ, for Paul, being engaged by an erroneous conscience, consented to the death of Stephen. Yes, could he, in that condition, have met with Jesus Christ Himself, he would have done the same against Him.

The fourth is the conversations of men. Heresy is seldom or never divided from impiety. Hymenaeus, who made shipwreck of the faith, made shipwreck also of a good conscience. Those whom Paul called "dogs" he also called "evil workers." And, in another place, speaking of some whose minds were defiled, he adds, and reprobate to every good work. Our Savior, speaking of false prophets, said, "You may know them by their fruits." The lives of men are consonant to the judgments of men. Truth and goodness are reciprocal, and so are falsehood and wickedness. The doctrine of faith is a doctrine of holiness too. And the doctrine of lies is the doctrine of profaneness too. He who falls from truth to falsehood will quickly fall from piety to wickedness. Truth is of a reforming virtue as well as of an informing nature. It salts and seasons both heart and life; but that error which putrefies the heart will putrefy the life also. The plague will, at length, rise and break out into blanes and blotches.

They who write the story of the Anabaptists begin it with error in their judgments, but end it with wickedness in their practices. And Cyprian, writing long since of Novatus, that pestilent heretic, said of him that he was one who itched after a few notions, and was beyond measure covetous, intolerably proud, no man so treacherous. He would commend you before your face, but cut your throat behind your back; as false a person as ever lived, a very firebrand who did not care what became of truth or peace. He turned the world upside down so that he might carry on his opinion.

The apostle, speaking of Antichrist, calls him that man of sin, no such sinner as he. Lyranus expounds it as one totally given up to sin, and Theophylact calls him "the ringleader of sin." And truly, it is most just with God to give them up to corrupt lives who, rejecting His truth, have given up themselves to corrupt errors and lies.

2. Heresies are a drowning and overwhelming flood. A flood, you know, is such a collection, such a heightening confluence of waters, as swells the rivers above their bounds and lays all under water. Now, there are three things which heresies overwhelm.

One is the glory of all glories, the glorious name of God, the glorious name of Christ, the glorious name of the Holy Spirit, the glorious name of divine truths. Heresy turns the glory into a lie. It gives God the lie, and Christ the lie, and the Holy Spirit the lie, for it gives truth the lie, the Scriptures the lie, which are the glory of God, and Christ, and the Holy Spirit. He who makes the Word of God a liar makes God Himself a liar.

O sirs! What is God without truth? And what is all the goodness of the gospel without truth? And what is all the fabric of man's salvation without truth? Truth is, as it were, the pin, the clasp, the knot that ties all. Pull out that, untie and break that, the excellencies of

God, the glories of Christ, the sweetness of the promises, the souls of men, the salvation of men's souls, all are dashed, are broken, are gone. And such work heresy makes. It dissolves the bond of all glory, yes, it resolves God into worse than nothing. No God is better than a false god. There is an open or secret blasphemy in all heresies. No man can condemn the truth of God, but in that he must likewise condemn the God of truth.

The second is the glory of religion. Religion is clipped and darkened. It grows low and beggarly when it is patched with error. It is a debasing of the gold to marry it with any metal of a courser birth. All religion is so much more excellent by how much more truth it has; but, when once it is adulterated, when once it is tainted and leavened with damnable errors, now the silver is become dross; the glory is departed from it. When a religion is like Nebuchadnezzar's image, part clay and part iron, it becomes low and contemptible. If the mixture of human inventions abates its glory, what an impairing is the mixture of corrupt, poisonous, and faith-subverting doctrines?

The third is not only the dignity, but also the very vital entity of a Church. Truth is the soul of that body, and falsehood is death to it. Schisms do much harm, but nothing like vile doctrines. Schisms only rent the coat, but heterodoxies rent the heart. Those pluck up the fence, but these pull down the building. Those tear away the children's lace, but these bereave the children of their bread. Those are a turbulent sea; these are a dead sea. Those scratch, but these kill. Men talk much of unchurching, and of Antichrist, and the limbs of Antichrist, but a church is never more near to giving up the ghost than when it is most near to giving up the truth. It is never nearer to being unchurched, and to be essentially Antichristed, than when the truth fails, and when abominable heresies and corrupt doctrines swarm in it. Mark seriously that place in 1 John 4:3, "Every spirit that confesseth not that Christ is come in the flesh is not of God, and this is that spirit of Antichrist." Yes, this is that spirit of Antichrist. That spirit of error and false doctrine is the spirit of Antichrist.

3.   Heresies are a sudden rising flood. A flood is no sober or quiescent puddle, no grave or slow-paced river, but it is a quick and extemporary collection and inundation. And, truly, in this lies the greatness of the danger to a people and Church by heresies. They are quickly conceived and quickly

brought forth; quickly born and quickly thriving. Truth, however, gets on very slowly by reason of that incapacity of the judgment for supernaturals, and by reason of that natural opposition in man to the things of God, and by reason of the subtle interposition of the prince of darkness, who blinds the minds of men, lest the light of the glorious gospel should shine to them.

Yet erroneous and false opinions break out with ease and spread swiftly. They are like the plague, which is a flying arrow. There needs no preparation of the ground for nettles. If the seeds merely drop down, you will soon have a full crop, yet the ground must be prepared again and again to receive good seed. The hearts of men are as naturally disposed to suck in errors as they are to send out wickednesses. The tinder is so prepared to catch the fire that it is but the striking of the flint and the work is done.

The Scriptures compare false doctrines to leaven. O how fast does a little leaven sour the lump! Paul wondered that the Galatians were so soon removed to another gospel, Galatians 1:6. The good man slept but one night, and the field was sown all over with tares by the wicked and envious man.

How quickly did the world turn Arian? How suddenly did the Anabaptists endanger Germany? The vines which have been some months in growing are in very few hours torn down and destroyed by foxes and wild boars.

Now, if erroneous doctrines are, in themselves, so pernicious, and in their operation so speedily diffusive, then certainly they are of all other things the most dangerous to the Church of Christ. A plague which suddenly infects many families is, therefore, the more dangerous; and heresies, which can suddenly infect many souls, are therefore the more dangerous evils.

4.   Heresies are an increasing and swelling flood. A flood at first makes the river only to look big, and to run a little thicker and faster; but, after a while, it causes the river to be unruly, to break in pieces, to super-abound. The waters contribute on every side and at every corner to raise and mount so that there is no passing. False doctrines, at first, seem to be modest. They will be but questions and queries, and then they come to be probabilities, and then they come to be tolerable conclusions, and then they rise to be unquestionable tenets, and then are fit to be made

public articles, and then are necessary to be held, and then the contrary is not to be maintained or spoken for, no, to be disdained and reproached.

But this is not all either; for, as false opinions rise thus, and increase in their direct line of particular magnitudes by way of intention, so they likewise enlarge themselves in diverse breadths by way of extension. They are like circles in a pond. One circle begets another. So one heresy begets another; a lesser begets a greater. As one moral sin is but a stair to step down lower, so this intellectual sin of heresy is but a stair to help up to higher and worse errors.

If you will consult historical antiquity, it is wonderful to behold the great flames bred out of small sparks. What monstrous opinions have been built upon errors which seemed but little at the first. How one error has hatched a greater! They who write of them can distinctly tell us where the man was first planet-struck (what his first error was); but, after a while, they are nonplussed in the account. The number of errors has doubled and tripled, such a maze and labyrinth is error. It is like a whirlpool which first sucks in one part and then another, and never desists until it draws in and plunges the whole body.

Besides ancient examples, we may see this swelling growth of erroneous opinions in the Church of Rome, where one error still advanced to more errors, and those again to higher errors, and these still ran on until a general corruption ensued from all the particulars. Compare the first defections and corruptions with their last and present. How little then, how total now; how particular then, how universal now. And you will easily acknowledge what increasing floods erroneous opinions are.

The points, at first, were rather about private interests of precedence, but they have so increased to all things doctrinal that they are scarcely found in any. Their errors about the Scriptures and traditions, about the offices of Christ, about human satisfaction and merits, about invocation and adoration of saints, about justification and faith, about good works, about freewill, about the Sacraments, are evident to the entire world.

I could give you an instance also in the Anabaptists in Germany, whose first author there (said David Chytraeus, in his Dedicatory Epistle to Ericus, King of the Swedes), was Nicolaus Pelargus Cygneus, about the year 1523. His erroneous doctrines, though bad enough, for they were laid in the contempt of the ministry of the Word and Sacraments, and rejection of the civil magistrate, yet were not formerly so numerous, but when these opinions descended to Thomas Munzer and Andreas Carlstadt, then they began to swell both in the quantity of the opinions, and in the vast number of disciples too.

Lambertus Danaeus, in his annotations and explications of St. Augustine's book De Haeresibus & Quod Vult Deum, adds to that account the many derivations and enlarging propogations of heresies from age to age, showing exactly the several heresies flowing from some one capital and original heresy, as from Simon Magus's heresy, and from that of Valentinus, and that of Cardo, and that of Artemon, and that of Novatus, and that of Arius, *etc.* In that elaborate work of his, you may read of such a strange growth of heresies that they never stopped multiplying and breeding until they had (as much as in them lay), overthrown and cashiered every person in the Trinity: all the Scriptures, the Law and the gospel, every distinct moral commandment, every particular article of faith, every ordinance of Jesus Christ, the preaching of the Word, baptism, the Lord's Supper, *etc.*

There are four general heads to which, usually, we reduce the Christian religion: (1) The Decalogue of the Law; (2) The symbol of faith; (3) The Lord's Prayer; and (4) the Sacraments. And that learned author, Danaeus, by name instances the several heretical, erroneous teachers who have invaded every one of these, and in every particular comprehended in them, by all which it most clearly appears how dangerously mischievous heretical opinions are to the Church of God.

5.   There is one more thing which I would add in the last place, by which it shall be manifested that these heretical opinions are more dangerous than any other floods, and that is a diverse quality in them. Other floods are quickly up and quickly down. Although they grew high and perilous, there is a sudden transiency in the height and peril. Their principles are unconstant though violent and, being spent, these ordinary floods sink and famish for want of supply and feeding. But the floods of false and erroneous doctrines are such as quickly rise, but very slowly abate. They are, in this respect, worse than the great deluge in the days of Noah, which continued

many months, but then slacked and sank, and fell quite away.

It is not so with heretical errors; they are like diseases which come upon us flying, but go away from us creeping. Some erroneous opinions have been kept up for forty years together, no, above one hundred years together, some of them for three hundred years.

O brethren! Men dote on their own fancies; they are exceedingly pleased with their own brats, especially with the new concepts of their own minds. They dearly like them, love them, and foster them. For one heretic who has been poisoned in his judicials, you will find a thousand others converted and reduced who have only been stained in their morals. Heresy, or the heretical opinion, is described of by all the parts, arguments, shifts, learning of carnal reason, and it is born up by a haughty, disdainful, and proud spirit. And it is so fallacious and fraudulent, when you come to handle it, and it is so rammed in with obstinacy and peremptoriness, that it is almost a miracle to work effectually on a heretic.

Every heretic is odiously proud. All other men who dissent from him are far below him, and one said very truly, "No proud man can endure to be accounted a fool or a knave." So simple as to be deceived or so base as to deceive, one of which the heretic thinks he must take to his share if at any time he recants his heretical and seducing doctrine.

I should now come to show to you the reasons why Satan makes use of this dangerous flood against the Church, and why especially at some times more than others. He knows well that there remains in professing Christians many advantages for him as to erroneous opinions, much ignorance, much pride and self-conceitedness, much itching vanity, much vain glory, much faternal envy, much carelessness and inadvertency, *etc.*, but I must wave this and conclude all with some seasonable applications to ourselves.

APPLICATION

USE 1. Are heresies, erroneous and false doctrines, such a dangerous and pernicious flood to the Church of God? Is there so much sinfulness in them? So much dishonor to Christ? So much injury to the truth of God? So much hazard to the immortal souls of men? O, then, what just, what sad, what singular cause do all of us have this day to enlarge our tears and humiliations? There are many floods which call for our tears: the flood of innocent blood in Ireland; the flood of cries from poor widows and orphans; the flood of needy and wounded soldiers, and there is yet another flood, a worse flood, the flood of heresies and blasphemies. One deep calls for another, the flood of wicked and ungodly opinions calls earnestly for a flood of sorrow and lamentation.

We are, by God's mercy and goodness, indifferently rescued from the cruelty of dragons. O, but now we are as much endangered with the flood of the serpent! The bodies of people are, in some good measure, secured from the edge of the sword; but what of this while the souls of people are hazarded with the poison of errors? If the danger flies from the body to the soul, if the corporal danger is exchanged for a spiritual danger, where is our happiness? What is our safety by this?

Beloved, there are four notable reasons for our most solemn humiliation for the spiritual wickednesses, for the false and abominable doctrines which, like a flood, are now overwhelming this nation.

I.   The account or height of some of them. They amount to no less than execrable blasphemies, to ignominious, contemptuous, disgraceful reproaches of God, Christ, and the Holy Scriptures. Believe me, blasphemy is a daring sin. It presses very close and too sore on God. "He that blasphemeth the name of the Lord, he shall surely be put to death," (Leviticus 24:16). The words according to the original are, "He that strikes through the name of Jehovah." Blasphemy is that bold sword which is hacking God Himself, which is, as it were, cleaving of Him asunder. The schoolmen tell us that blasphemy breaks out in three ways.

First, when we affirm that of God which is unbecoming of God, which is incompatible with His holy and divine nature; as to make Him a creature, a liar, or to make Him cruel, unjust, unmerciful, sinful, or the cause of sin.

Second, is when we deny that to God which indeed belongs to God. It is called blasphemy in the king of Assyria when he said that the Lord "was not able to deliver Jerusalem out of his hand," (2 Chronicles 32:17).

Third, is when we put that on the creature which is proper to God. So, when the Israelites had made a molten calf and said, "This is thy God that brought thee up out of Egypt, it is added that they brought great provocations," (Nehemiah 9:18). In the Hebrew it is, "And they committed great blasphemies."

Now, compare this short discourse of the kinds of blasphemies with the many expressions that fall in the speeches of some, and set down in the writings of others, and then judge whether some of our modern errors do not rise as high as blasphemy.

1.   That God is the author of sin; not only of the actions to which sin cleaves, but of the very sinfulness itself: of the disorderliness, depravity, and irregularity.

2.   That the saints in this life are fully perfect, as omniscient as God.

3.   That the fullness of the Godhead dwells bodily in every saint in the same measure as it did in Christ Jesus while He was here on earth.

4.   That when the fullness of the Godhead shall be manifested in the saints, then they shall have more power than Christ had, and do greater works than He did, and that they shall then have divine honor.

5.   And one has been complained of for saying that Jesus Christ was a bastard.

6.   Another said that he was Jesus Christ, the Messiah.

7. That Jesus Christ is not God essentially, but nominally.

8. That His human nature was defiled with original sin like ours.

9. That He is not of a holier nature than men.

10. That it is as possible for Jesus Christ to sin as it is for a child of God to sin.

11. That there is no such thing as the Trinity of Persons.

12. That the Scriptures are but of human invention, a mere shadow, a false history, and ought not to be the foundation of any man's faith any more than the Apocrypha and other books, *etc.*

When Hezekiah heard the blasphemies of Rabshakeh, he rent his clothes, covered himself with sackcloth, went into the house of the Lord, and sent to the prophet Isaiah, saying, This is a day of trouble, and of rebuke, and of blasphemy. That day of blasphemy was a day of trouble and vexation to him. Though the blasphemy was from an Assyrian, yet it was a day of trouble to him. And what should the day be to us when it is a day of many blasphemies, and that not from professed Assyrians, but from professing Christians?

What Christian can hear, can bear, such indignities and reproaches cast upon his God and his Christ without a bleeding and rising spirit?

II.   The breadth or number of false and erroneous opinions. So many and so grievous! Verily, they grow so thick, so abundant, that they will leave us neither Church nor state, neither ministry nor ordinances, neither duties nor worship. There are some who have printed large catalogues of them; I will but pick a few of the more notorious of them and spread them before you this day.

1.   The   Scriptures of the Old Testament do not bind us Christians, nor those of the New Testament either, any further than the Spirit (for the present), reveals to us that such a place is the Word of God.

2.   That God never loved one man more than another before the world, and that the decrees are all conditional.

3.   That there is no original sin.

4.   That the will of man is still free, even to things that are supernatural.

5.   That the saints may fall totally and finally from grace.

6. That Christ died alike for all, yes, that the salvific virtue of His death extends to all reprobates as well as to the elect, yes, to the very devils as well as to men.

7. That Jesus Christ came into the world not for satisfaction, but for publication; not to procure for us, and to us, the love of God, but only to be a glorious Publisher of the gospel.

8. That God is not displeased at all if His children sin, and it is no less than blasphemy for a child of God to ask pardon for his sins.

9. That sanctification is a dirty and dungy qualification.

10. That the doctrine of repentance is a soul destroying doctrine.

11. That fastings and humblings are legal and abominable.

12. That the souls of men are not immortal but mortal.

13. That there is no heaven to crown the godly and no hell to torment the ungodly.

14. That civil magistracy is anti-Christian, and but a usurpation.

15.   That the whole ministry of the land, as to their present ordination and standing is anti-Christian.

16.   That it is as lawful to baptize cats and dogs and horses (which some have done for some of them, if not for all and more), as it is to baptize the infants of believers.

17.   That there is no true ministry this day in all the world, nor was since the general apostasy which, they say, began since the death of the last of the Apostles.

18.   That there will be no ministry either until some apostles are raised up and sent; and, when those apostles come, then there will be true evangelists also, and pastors, and not until then. Hearken, O people, and judge, O Christians, whether the serpent has not cast out his flood among us! Judge whether the errors in our times do not call for more high thoughts and more deep tears.

III.   Let me make a note on the length or peril by all these. If the peril were confined only to the souls of them who are the craftsmen and founders of these opinions, yet even this should move us to lament; but the flood is running, the water is spreading. The plague is not only begun but wasting; the contagion grows to be general. It has gotten into the city, into the country, it has gotten into that (other) chief university. The poison is dropped into the springs. It has gotten into many leaders of the people who themselves err, and cause others to err. It breathes; it walks, and rolls up and down. It is spreading over the whole kingdom. It surprises place after place, infects family after family. The sword of late was not so swift to conquer bodies, as errors are now to poison souls.

Truly, sirs! If blasphemies against God; if reproaches against Christ; if decisions against the Holy Spirit; if contempt of the Scriptures; if vilifying of the ordinances of Christ; if abuses to our holy profession; if the eternal hazard of souls; if all of these cannot affect or afflict us, I do not know what to say to you!

IV.   The special engagements which are on us all to lay all these things with sorrow to our hearts.

Beloved! We are Christians (let others think of us as they please); we are covenanting Christians (let others deride this as they will); and we are, or should be, penitent Christians (let others be what they please), now.

Consider us as Christians. We take ourselves to be the children of the true and living God and profess ourselves to be the members of Jesus Christ. The faith of Christ is delivered to us. We are entrusted with it; we are responsible for it; we are to be zealous for it. How, then, can we suffer our God, our Christ, our faith, to be thus dishonorably injured and abused, and not be troubled at all!

Consider us as covenanting Christians. So we have, every one of us, bound our souls to God. Can any mortal creature here release us? We have lifted up our hands to the Most High God in our several places to extirpate heresies and false doctrines.

Yes, consider us as penitent Christians. Fasting Christians should be so; they should be mourning Christians. And Christians who penitentially mourn will mourn for the sins of others as well as for their own sins. And they will mourn most when God is dishonored most. And can God be dishonored more than by blasphemies and damnable heresies? Put all of these together, and then consider whether these sins of heresies and blasphemies should not wound our souls with grief, which have wounded our God with so much dishonor.

USE 2. But I pass from this use of humiliation to a second use, which shall be for exhortation, and it is this: since there is such a flood cast out of the mouth of the serpent to carry away the woman, let us carefully improve the following words in the text, "And the earth helped the woman, and opened her mouth to swallow up the flood." Before I distribute my exhortation, let me premise a distinction or two.

There is a twofold opening of the mouth concerning this flood. One is to speak for damnable errors and opinions, and such as vent and maintain them. O, that the mouth of any Christian should ever open itself on behalf of those who dare open their mouths in blasphemy against their God and Christ! Should the welfare of a corrupt and poisonous seducer be dearer to you than the glory of your God, than the truth of your Savior?

But there is another opening of the mouth, and that is against damnable errors and heresies. "We can do nothing against the truth, but for the truth," said Paul. "Contend earnestly for the faith once delivered to the saints," said Jude. Hold fast the faithful Word, for there are many unruly and vain talkers and deceivers, whose mouths must be stopped, who "subvert whole houses," *etc.*, so the apostle says in Titus 1:9-11.

Again, there is a twofold swallowing up of this flood. One is by way of impression and furtherance, of imitation and countenance. Like the fish that swallows the bait, too many swallow up the flood in this sense: The prophets prophesy falsely, and my people love to have it so, Jeremiah 5:31. There shall be false teachers, who privily shall bring in damnable heresies, and many shall follow their "pernicious ways," 2 Peter 2:12.

Another is by way of hindrance and repression, so as to make the danger of this flood to sink and cease. O, bring in your help! Bring it in fully; bring it in speedily in this way to swallow up this flood. Believe it; if you do not carefully swallow up this flood, this flood will, not long after, swallow you up, and this kingdom too.

Now, there are two sorts of men especially who may help, and who ought to help swallow up and repress the present flood of heresies and blasphemies.

1. You, right honorable men, and the rest who are Christian magistrates. It was but the scornful speech of Tiberius that the gods alone must remedy the injuries offered to them. O no! You are guardians of

each table of the law. You are designed to be the nursing fathers. You have received the sword to be a terror to evil. Pious and learned William Ames, speaking to the question as to whether heretics are to be punished by the civil magistrate, answered in this way, "The position and duty of the magistrate demands that he repress shameless disturbers with the sword, or by public external power if there is need." It is his place and duty to repress and restrain them if they are noxious and turbulent. Yes, and he adds, more than everyone will be patient to hear; namely, that if also they are manifestly blasphemous and pertinacious, they may be cut off by capital punishment, according to Leviticus 24:15-16. But I will not fall upon the discussion of this at this time. All that I would humbly suggest to you is this, that you may help against the dangerous flood nine ways.

1)   By a peremptory abhorring and crushing of that flood-begetting maxim, viz. a catholic liberty and toleration of all opinions. There was a religion (as one spoke before you), of all gods among the old Romans, and there is a religion of all saints now among the Papists. And, if the serpent could but wriggle in a religion of all opinions among the English, he needs to

desire no more. If men can step from one religion on to all, they will soon fall from all religion to none.

2) By a public declaration against all heresies and blasphemies known to be spoken and printed. When Ostorodius and Vaidovius started out their Socinian heterodoxies in the low countries, the States General packed away those seducers with exile, and publically condemned and committed their pestiferous books to the fire.

3) By making some standing laws against such opinions, which can be proved to be heretical and blasphemous. One has said, "Kings of the earth serve Christ also by passing laws in Christ's interest."

4) By setting up your church discipline with full power, so that it may reach these heresies and blasphemies, which, if any sins, then they plainly fall within the verge of it. If the discipline were fully and generally established, you should not have a heresy or blasphemy or any erroneous opinion creeping out in any part of the kingdom, but there would be a timely discovery of it; and, likewise, a spiritual remedy to recover erring persons and to prevent their further spreading.

5)   By encouraging and heartening the godly, orthodox, ministers of the gospel in their assertings and vindicatings of the truths of God, and in their oppugning of wicked, dangerous, and damnable opinions; not suffering the ministers to be snibbed, abused, reviled, scorned, slandered, disturbed, or hazarded because they oppose the adversaries of truth, and those serpents which cast out floods among us. Why should the shepherd be discouraged because he keeps wolves from the sheep? Or why should any man be checked because he would quench the flying fire?

6)   By using your prudent authority in a timely causing of faithful and able ministers to be sent forth; such as are thoroughly tried and well-approved to be sound in the faith, and skillful to convince gainsayers and seducers. The more you help truth, and the servants of truth, the more you help in this to contribute against errors and the enemies of truth. There is no better help against darkness than light.

7)   By a tender and watchful eye to the universities, one of which is lately fallen into your possession. Take care that it does not fall into the possession of any seducers. You have heard, no doubt, of a late disputation in Oxford where somebody

undertook to maintain (besides in private), divers strange and dangerous opinions in public. I humbly entreat you to take care that the serpent does not get in his body before there is any planted to bruise his head. Truth by right is the firstborn, and should inherit first. Do not put the truth to play an after-game with error. Other garrisons, if lost, may easily be reduced, but that which is surprised fast by error is not so easily recovered.

8)   By enjoining a solemn day of humiliation through all the land for the dishonors redounding to God, Christ, and the truth, by the present errors, heresies, and blasphemies. Lately, you did so for the floods of rain which endangered the corn. O, that it might seem good to you to do so for the flood of errors which endanger souls! This humble request I presume to leave with your pious zeal and prudence.

9)   By using your coercive power with such methods and proportions as the real safety of truth and souls requires, and the repression of dangerous errors needs. So managing the distributions thereof that, under the notion of restraining heresy, you by no means injure real sanctity, nor yet, under the pretense of sanctity, you do not favor the growth of heresy. O, what

a happy people are they among whom errors are losing and truths are gaining! Where piety thrives and wickedness blasts! Where all who are good can join against all that is evil and, in lesser things, whereas yet they cannot (through weakness), clasp opinions; yet (for the truth and peace's sake), can clasp hearts and hands to promote God's glory and the common salvation of souls!

2. I have a word also to say to you who are ministers of the gospel of Christ. Come forth from your long silences, neglects, and reserves. Help the Church of Christ in swallowing up the flood which the serpent has cast out of his mouth. "When Jesus Christ is blasphemed, it is not a time to fear, but to cry out!" said Luther to Staupitius. Men will say that you are moderate and discreet, but what will Christ say to you, if at such a time you are silent in His cause?

O, my brethren! You are the husbandmen; take heed that no one sows tares in the field while you sleep. You are the builders; O, be sure to preserve the foundation safe! You are the shepherds of the flock; O beware of the wolves lest they break in and destroy the sheep! You are the vinedressers and keepers of the vineyard; O, have an eye to the foxes who will otherwise spoil the tender grapes! You are the stewards of Christ; O, be vigilant on what provision the household feeds! You are the watchmen; O, look out lest the enemy slip in and surprise the city! You are the fathers; be sure that your children do not have a stone given to them instead of bread, or a serpent instead of a fish.

You must help with your most fervent prayers, as Alexander once did and prevailed against Arius. You must help with your counsels, with your watchings, with your preachings. You must *bona docere & mala de docere*, as Austin says. You must stand for truth and withstand errors. You are, in a singular manner, entrusted with truth and souls. O, watch! O, pray! O, preach! O, do all that faithful ministers should do when a flood breaks in!

You read of Elijah's zeal against the false prophets, and Paul's zeal against false apostles. You have read of the zeal of Athanasius against the Arians, and of the zeal of Cyprian against the Novatians, and of the zeal of Austin against the Donatists, the Manichees, and the Pelagians. You have read of the zeal of Jerome, of Chrysostom, of Nazianzen, and many others in ancient times. You have read of the zeal of Luther and

Calvin, and others in later times. You have showed your zeal to the kingdom in dangerous times.

I say no more. Remember your first works; remember your engagements, and be zealous. If you who are the angels of Christ, the ministers of Christ, the stewards of Christ, if you are drowsy, if you are silent, if you stop your own mouths when mouths are opened against Christ, whose mouth can we expect should open itself to swallow up the flood? It was a brave answer which Cyril gave to Theodosius that, in our private and personal injuries, we should hold our peace; but, when the truth (or faith) is in danger of being corrupted, we ought to speak, else we must give an account to God of our unseasonable silence.

USE 3. I have one use more. Has the serpent cast out such a flood of errors and false doctrines among us?

1.   Then let everyone take heed lest he be carried away with any part of this flood. I say, take heed; for erroneous times are trying times and proving times as well as bloody and persecuting times. God has tried your fidelity to this kingdom of late by a flood of blood, and God is now trying your fidelity to the kingdom of His dear Son by a flood of errors. Take heed lest you be carried away by this flood.

There are seven things which are very apt to be carried away by a flood: light things, loose things, weak things, low things, rotten things, tottering things, and venturous things. O, take heed:

1)   That you are not light or proud Christians. Errors are most apt to breed in a proud brain and a graceless heart; and no man is more likely to be overturned by error than he who has overturned himself by pride. The *proud* and *blasphemers* are joined together, 2 Timothy 3:2. The proud man is exposed to most temptations, to most falls, and to most errors. It is the proud man who does not consent to wholesome words of Christ, but dotes about questions, 1 Timothy 6:34.

2)   That you are not loose Christians. If ungodliness is in the heart, it will not be hard for error to get into the head. A loose heart can best comply with loose principles. Truth is searching and reforming, but error is more quiet and gratifying. It is grace which settles the mind and establishes the heart.

3)   That you are not weak Christians. Weak stomachs are most longing. A Christian whose faith is implicit and leaning on man often trusts out his judgment and soul. The weaker light you have of truth,

the more easily you may be cheated with errors instead of truth.

4)   That you are not low Christians. A worldly heart is a very low heart. It is, of all others, the cheapest. It will be bought and sold upon every turn to serve its own turn. The truth can never be sure in that chest which any error with a little golden key can pick. If you are the servant of truth for gain, you will be a slave to error for more gain.

5)   That you are not rotten or hypocritical Christians. They were given up to believe lies who did not receive the truth in the love of it. How just is it with God that he should fall into real error whose heart never loved real truth? That the deceitful heart should at length be a deceived heart? Is it difficult to set him against the faith who never had a sound faith?

6)   Take heed that you are not tottering and unstable Christians. When the judgment is not balanced and solidly fixed upon the truths of Christ, but reeling and wavering and, like those in Elijah's time, halting between two opinions, it is usually in danger to be poised with error. He whose mind is but indifferent about a truth is more than half on his way to error.

7)   Take heed that you are not venturous or soul-tempting Christians. Julian slipped in his apostasy by going to hear Libanius. The devil is ready enough to tempt you; do not be forward to tempt him. Eve lost all by hearing one sermon from the mouth of the serpent. If you will be trading among cheaters, it is no wonder if you are cheated. We are sure to go by the worst when we venture upon our own strength. The man who exposes himself to hear new truths oftentimes comes back with old errors newly dressed.

2.   Let everyone strengthen his soul that he may stand and withstand, and not be carried away. The house built on the rock stood when the flood came. Take all in a word: A judgment solidly principled, a heart sincerely renewed, a faith truly bottomed, truth and love of it cordially matched; profession and practice well-joined, a fear of ourselves and dependence upon God still maintained, God's ordinances and the society of humble and growing Christians still frequented, watchfulness and prayer still continued are the best directives that I can deliver to keep us in the truth, and the best preservatives that I know to keep us from error.

FINIS

www.ingramcontent.com/pod-product-compliance
Lightning Source LLC
Chambersburg PA
CBHW032005080426
42735CB00007B/517